JOKER'S GHOST

Leon J Gratton

Grosvenor House
Publishing Limited

The right of Leon J Gratton to be identified as the author of this
work has been asserted in accordance with Section 78
of the Copyright, Designs and Patents Act 1988

The front cover image is copyright to
www.istockphoto.com/gb/portfolio/nezezon2

The back cover image is copyright to
www.istockphoto.com/gb/portfolio/sedmak

This book is published by
Grosvenor House Publishing Ltd
Link House
140 The Broadway, Tolworth, Surrey, KT6 7HT.
www.grosvenorhousepublishing.co.uk

A CIP record for this book
is available from the British Library

ISBN 978-1-78623-073-7

Silent Quiet is
The night
No music
No drugs
Only my soul
That at least bugs
I have no way
Of dressing up in Love
I miss all my Friends
My lovers
The girls of every Weather

———

There is an angel
Crying over me
There is an angel
Crying over me
Who planted this?
Beautiful seed
She reminds me
I'm me
There's an angel
Crying over me

———

Dark raven hair
With the right look
You can't do nothing
But care
She looks dangerous
A brand new year's bride`　　　`
Hoping she has a Friend
At least whom I can set aside
Honey nuptials that
Smell of coffee out the tin
My head bangs like hell
And I think I've made
A new friend

There is nothing
More sinister
Than punishing
Yourself with
Flesh

———

Small face of relaxation
Taking tears of affection
Interested in love and direction
Small as the night is long
And no objection

———

My heart bound
In this Mortal Shackle
With grace of god
Evil we tackle
Take form Shadow
Turn us into the courage
We truly are

———

The next best thing
Since cocaine
The next best thing
Since cocaine
It's beautiful as summer
Rain
The next best thing
Since cocaine
And there's an angel
Crying over me
The style and comfort
Free
There's an angel crying
Over me
The distance we go
Is sweet
The next best thing
Since cocaine
Lullaby

Love the arrow
Love the nib
Love the carriage
Love the gift
Love is beautiful
Love is plain
Love conquers
Love can be tamed

———

My sign in this world
A guild masters worth
Smiling gently
I cast a begging eye
Or at least give me
A chance to scry
Set numbers
Set to craft
Set in sentence
To the very last

Smiling thru our
Eyeballs
Drinking all the time
Every chance we get
We do another line
The love bestowed
On our face
Left us with tequila lime

Dead is innocence
Only the whispers
Of love survive

———

A dragon is filled with
A thousand tears
With higher hand
And overseers

———

Blind tears
Shallow seers
Smiling men
Whose blood is in?
The pen
Wander far
Looking for a holy
Star
Love and peace
When we become
Intrigued
I have seen the world
At peace

I was summoned to life
And given the wonders
Of the heavens
She smiled sweetly
Said "hello" and the
People of my stance
Said take it real slow
The goddess slipped
In beside me
So I could recharge
For a while

Giants are close
To our illusion

———

We smile knowing
That we may be
Ending our integrity

———

My main man
Takes off in the
Way of Chan
My sniper training
Watch as I can
Follow follow and
Evade
Snake battle

Forever curled in her
Hair
Smiling eyes that
Forever share
Her lips red and hair of
Ember
Oh a darling that
I will always remember

———

The sun with no way of losing
My heart don't make me choose
Daybreak tripping I sing the blues
It's on spring with warm weather
Yes Janice It's you love adorns
My heart pumps for you
You are the lady I remember the
Most
Whilst turn of moon wax and wane
You know it's only when somethings
Wrong I complain
The colour of silk
The lace
The cooling breeze
I long to see your face

The burn with light
My coming will never happen
They arise with certain
Fever running and running
Never faithful to our
Own treasure
Our passion our demise
Into the boredom of an empty life
They never feel the fever grow upon them

My sweet success is when we become
Caught in the fondness of sweet Jane
I can't wait for the road to open its
Gemlike existence
Heaven

My love is always there
The angel made a move
To turn twist
Then soothe

When my heart smiles
And answers my prayers
Then life will turn
Us into the natural order
Of things
I know my mind on this and
Its
Deep Deep
Dragons keep

Lions roar
And tigers play
Love is a journey
And I smile at
Its way
We hold out
In jungle wisdom
We make our belief
Out of god's kingdom
It's everlasting
And holy of asking
Quiet night
Quiet night
Loves divine right

The soldier of the street war
Should clutch tightly to his
Soul
As he should know this
The immortal soul holds in it
The spark of resilience

———

The absolute beauty of souls
Lady you truly have a secret smile
And a heavenly garden
The night brings you to rest
A secret invitation begins in the way
You are

———

Promised gateway
Open pathway
Gentle mirror of the soul
A quiet golden treaty
Between you and me
We shine more and more
Someone stand by my side

———

Beneath our tranquillity
We swim towards our dreams
The dancing of our hearts
Which come together at the seams
The art of soul searching
Brings out the test to be
Truly humble

———

Soldier's poets and rebels
All go into the Skeleton world
Of night
Wise angel and Gods watch
Over us all
My honey come
And begin winter weather
I tell the tale, streets and battlefields
Of love

———

When arising and dreams
Close in our souls
Each one wept into the night
The terrible ocean over the heavens

———

There is in the darkest shadows
An immortal psychic sexual
Organ making day solemn
And hot, And night fiery as any sun
The angels take my beating heart and soul
Love you Laura

———

My only Life
The night flying high
It's considered
It's a well being
The soul marches on
Soldier carnage and gold
Will you smile at this?
Hero of the unfortunate

———

My spine closed the spirit
And racked my very own religion
Gods of beauty love of soul
My one mind
My one body
Quietly I give religion to my heart
And cancel the devils toll

———

Soft sugar bubbles
In love with a little heart
And turning away
From the sun
I smile when I think of your love
And turn back to bubble gum

———

It's the wonder of the Drug trade
A woman to over play
The Sun with presents
Everyway
The sound colliding
With the stars
Gone to oriental play

Fight with love and
Honour on your side
Trace back to beauty
And wonder

The silent moreish way
Of the divine soul
In eternity the soldiers
Patrol

My heart shed there
And marmalade
Does some strange things
Puts in the appearance
Then shows you how to live
My friends keep running
With drugs and drink
I'm clean doesn't
That make you think

I got a ring on my finger
I got a string on my soul

I believe in you sister
And I will live
For rock and roll
I got a habit
Like the pope
Years and years old

My guiding star
Which is helpful
I can take on
The paper doll

I got a ring on my finger
I got a radiant soul

I got love with my sisters and brothers
And Know that god could end us all

Well the fever starts running when
I test the mettle in my soul
Well magic save me lord
As the world is to slow

I got a ring on my
Finger
But never mix your silver with gold

The lord of the hunt
Save me
From the bottomless
Hole
The next time we
Meet I'll tell you about
The jelly roll

———

The soul boasts resilience
Whilst angels go on patrol
Looking for an enemy
Foreign then cashing
In at the dole

———

Slaves to darkness
Saints to wisdom
Show me a spell about love
No kiss and tell
Wonder
Wonder
Why this ink
Is blue
Heroes to light

———

Strangeness comes but once a year
When shadows crawl in our fear
Ladies smile at winter cold
Love over death
Even the old

———

The first time I saw her, the very first time
She was looking at me with wonder in her
Eyes. And all I could think was am I that
Attractive surely not. But you lady queen are
Indeed hot. Have sweet delicious dreams

———

Love can make any wish come true
Love can show you things you never
Knew
My heart slowly
Breaking over you
But love will shine on
Gone the days of drugs and games
I'm sat here lonely
Aint that strange

———

Must bed down
Before I wed down
A smiling creature
Said to me
Don't exceed what
You think is excessive
Smile all the while
Cause the world and
Time we just visit
Envisioned in her
Beauty
Bangs a drum
Graceful Majestical
The prince of dragons
Carries on
After life and after
Death we present
Some, how else is this
World going to
Carry on

Align with love to the stars
Quiet see yourself
In beauty and wars
With nothing to keep you
Hanging in there
But the fact that
Love will win again

———

Good luck lover
Good night hero
Good rest gods
And bless us all
Forever going to crawl

———

Caged in hearts
Minus the regret
Lovers walk calm
Smile at the sweet
Air
Hold on to your angel
The silent mood
That love is
Comes near and far
Can you smile if you
See me with heartfelt
Distance
And stars bouncing of the seas

Abound by penniless hunger
Lustful games and quiet apples

The rock god smiled
With diamonds in his eyes
The steely stone
Dead cowboy
Has steel in his gaze
Love is wonderful

It's cold and dark
Turning of weather
Smile all the while
As heroes will treasure
A man
A lady
Should know each
Other better
Lovers be still

———

That white poppy
Humour
Being forgotten rumour
With shades of love
On the stage
Thanks Kylie
You're amazing in the platinum age

———

Man is but selling
A dream
To a worthy god

———

The half queen
The fair time
Sugar men come and go
Sugar men come and go
But candy stripe girls
Last forever

Moonlight Marble
With tattooed soul
The pillar of soul
Which turns to salt
At first sign of dawn
Quiet fix this sadness
As love adorns the sky
Which leaves us petty the
Gladness goes and we sigh
At brilliant stars
That adorn the sky

A feast of eyeballs
All summer
Whilst a libido
Toeing male
Keeps it sane

———

Smile on those of us
Who have neither?
Incline or wit to just
Walk on by
Week long beggar
Thief
Smoke on swords are
Sheathed
My moral time outside
The humour of life
Coming in and out
Like the moons reflection
On the sea

———

The night shows
Our heart polite
Ways to go and pick
A mile of trouble
The grain
The smile
The teacher teaches
All the while
Soon we will see
Our love let go
Let go
You deserve
This my son

Moonlight Marble
The star open sky
My heart will be black
With pain and regret
Then salt I shall
Become pilliard and
Tall
Go from venom
Smile at my hand
Love you all

———

A secret lawful entrance
Gave out a small hint
Of sex and all its many
Guises that hold my
Very eyes and summoned
The very beginning in this
Ancient land which will
Forever show touch and seduction
I smile at the little gardens
In heaven
That we follow through
With touch and freedom

Sun came out and I was
Scared over to the wrong
I watch as pristine thought
Comes over into our
Last dance at midnight

———

The air is sweet
And love is ever fonder
When we meet
My heart famished
When I don't see you
I smile as the soul needs
Glue

———

A silent scream
Getting taken
Back to the ladies dream
My heart has felt
The tender touch
Of both your eyes and soul

———

Blood and sister
Where do we go now?
Blood and sister
Half here and half allowed
Blood and sister
Where are you now
Blood and sister
I need you now
Blood and sister
We are not that proud

———

Sugar up a skirt and show me
Love
Love quietly with dark flowers
It's with dawn we see the towers

Sugar up a skirt
Sugar it up with no way of knowing
Sugar it up so I can flirt

Place the mist with sweet smelling nature
Eden holds nothing but birds and bees
Sugar up a skirt and show me
Your tease

Sugar up a skirt
Sugar it up with no way of knowing
Sugar up so I can see you up with
Out slowing

———

Is it just rust?
Or should I run away
The girls the children of freedom
Demi I heard you were game
But remember somethings
Done drive you Insane
Death is a touchy subject
When your blood aint
Tame

———

Show me one act of compassion
And I'll show you a thousand smiles

———

Promised gateway
Open pathway
Gentle mirror of the soul
A quiet golden treaty
Between you and me
We shine more and more
Someone stand by my side

———

Beneath our tranquillity
We swim towards our dreams
The dancing of our hearts
Which come together at the seams
The art of soul searching
Brings out the test to be
Truly humble

Standing in the ether of dreams
The true street soldier
With delicate humble beginnings
Our work never done
And my intrigue in dreams
And stars
Show parallel universes
But true love
Is fed into us and it makes
us lost to heart, mind and soul
Love forever

Burning up with drugs again
Burning up waiting for the rain
Torque the fuel give me the speed
Do you know the devil can you see
Him feed

———

Well well baby who hurts
The most
Well well lover can you see the
Jokers ghost

———

Hang me any way you can
Hang me and see pandemonium land
Upside down with halo burning up
Well hell in light whilst I light one up

The devil may care
But I don't give a damn

The devil may care
But I don't give a damn

The devil she smiled at me
I told her plain I'd
Rather drown at sea
Now rattle on drugs I
Might be

The devil may care
But I don't give a damn

I'd rather be a river
Baptist man
Smiling at the quiet
River Baptist man

———

Tranquilized deaths
Opium breathing breath
It's the world to some
Blonde hair
Lizard eyes that stare
Do it lady be my one

Well well it's here
Banded together
With opiate gear
I crush those pills
Put them in my coffee
Every day I watch the world
Fearful guests
Lizard hiss at dreams rests
My girl beautiful
With blonde hair
Yes yes the beauty is there
Please the day and the lord won

Well well its here banded together
With opiate gear
I crush those pills
Put them in my coffee
Everyday I watch the world

Valium opiate on the scene
Very confusing
Gone the scream
Oh oh cancerous child
Should be out there
Running wild

———

The scribe taking his time
The crossing over of mystical lines
See you there dark hair eyes as
Pure as time
My world quiet whilst I write these
Rhymes
Your face upset the stench of mind
Well places go on and love isn't
Blind
Time to die
Time to see
Time to live
Time to breathe

My love is always there
The angel made a move
To turn twist then soothe

Shame Shame I'm going hame
Broken leg mended
Tiger to be tamed
The silence
In a whisper
The enjoyment in
A game
Don't forget the
Dragons
As they are full of tears

I had once the sweet time
The subtle turn of brilliance
The silk in shine
My worldly resilience
The closing of this rhyme

———

How young we were
How cold they bare
My honor what is wrong
The lady is blue with a thong

———

While I'm gone
These words stay strong
Life is so mis-placed
My minor B flat baritone
Is set to the sassy Jazz hat
Never minding the
Rat-ta-tat
Love will come soon
Rum and coke
Havana style
The hairbrush yeah

Mr sand came round
Holding my attention
Mr sand came round
With holy invention
Mr sand smile
About an exception
Mr sand is me
With a bad ass
Reputation

A silent scream
Getting taken
Back to the ladies
Dream
My heart has felt
The tender touch
Of both your eyes
And soul

Its cold and dark
Turning of weather
Smile all the while
As heroes will treasure
A man
A lady
Should know each
Other better
Lovers be still

———

We bless

———

She smiles
Soft white
Suple face
Her eyes blue
Will capture you
The mask of love
Will make you a place
In her heart

How do I dress
My love down
Without being a clown
My heart beating
At your name
Which is sound

A childs heart
Hides a thousand
Smiles

Lions roar
And tigers play
Love is a journey
And I smile at its way
We hold out in the
Jungle wisdom
We make our Belief
Out of Gods kingdom
It's everlasting
And holy of asking
Quiet night
Quiet night
Loves divine right

They way of way
The chocolate high
Time slips its deadly tie
My mind shattering
Please don't cry
The angel running
From the storm
Hit miss
The nightime hiss

———

My only life
The night flying high
It's considerd
It's a well being
The soul marches on
Soldier carnage and gold
Will you smile at this
Hero of the unfortunate

———

My spine closed the spirit
And wracked my very own
Religion
Gods of beauty love of soul
My one mind
My one body
Quietly I give religion to my
Heart
And cancel the devils toll

———

She flies thru the night
Wrapping it's inky quality
Around her
He drowns himself in earths rain
And gentle weather
The gods smile at her as she swims
Thru the pin hole night
"she is your saviour"
Says a voice small but powerful
The gods are inviting us
A race of warlike fools
"Keep falling in love"
A goddess this time
She is pleasantly surprised
By the man's warm weather
That shows
The world comes to
Us all
But not everyman
Knows its power

My match met with
Quiet humour
It's a delicate path to take
With deeds of meer mortal souls
Many nights of quiet lunar despair
Calling on our sacrifice
To avenge the short lives we live
Quietly we go
Into the beating womb
Called heaven

———

Ghetto gives us the choice
Self anihlation or pray for better
Days Sad once for fools gold
Goes unnoticed
And the illicit substances like
Tuti- fruiti
See our minds and souls
Are playing for keeps
So children of the
Lunar food call again
Bye

Surely one of you ladies
Are a woman of substance
Quiet
I take that back
The angel in the storm
Is back smile

———

Small wonder
I contemplate a grand
Design
Into the arms of a new
Lover
With fire fueling
My soul
Imagery look onto
A sky of ink and light
The moon
Sad but glad
We didn't turn that way

———

Sun glowing gold and
Sending his dragon to rest
My time alive to help love
Rest tonight
And gentle in faith
Please
Please
Talk to me

Beneath our tranquillity
We swim towards our dreams
The dancing of our hearts
Which come together at the seams
The art of soul searching
Brings out the test to be
Truly humble

Into the shadows, they call me
Into the shadows, I turn the three
Into the shadows, the cards call
Into the shadows, I'm a devil enthralled

———

The night took hold
And ceremonies were sold
It's a life and death game I'm told

———

www.ingramcontent.com/pod-product-compliance
Lightning Source LLC
Chambersburg PA
CBHW022129280326
41933CB00007B/606